Searchlight BOOKS™

Space Mysteries

Mysteries of Black Holes

Margaret J. Goldstein

Lerner Publications ◆ Minneapolis

Lerner Publications Company
An imprint of Lerner Publishing Group, Inc.
241 First Avenue North
Minneapolis, MN 55401 USA

For reading levels and more information, look up this title at www.lernerbooks.com.

Main body text set in Adrianna Regular 14/20.
Typeface provided by Chank.

Designer: Mary Ross
Lerner team: Sue Marquis

Library of Congress Cataloging-in-Publication Data

Names: Goldstein, Margaret J., author.
Title: Mysteries of black holes / Margaret J. Goldstein.
Other titles: Searchlight books. Space mysteries.
Description: Minneapolis : Lerner Publications, [2021] | Series: Searchlight books - space mysteries | Includes bibliographical references and index. | Audience: Ages 8–11 | Audience: Grades 4–6 | Summary: "Readers curious about space will be fascinated by what astronomers currently know about black holes, and will learn about some of the mysteries we have yet to solve, in this high-interest STEM title"— Provided by publisher.
Identifiers: LCCN 2019053394 (print) | LCCN 2019053395 (ebook) | ISBN 9781541597402 (library binding) | ISBN 9781728413853 (paperback) | ISBN 9781728400860 (ebook)
Subjects: LCSH: Black holes (Astronomy)—Juvenile literature.
Classification: LCC QB843.B55 G65 2021 (print) | LCC QB843.B55 (ebook) | DDC 523.8/875—dc23

LC record available at https://lccn.loc.gov/2019053394
LC ebook record available at https://lccn.loc.gov/2019053395

Manufactured in the United States of America
1-47844-48284-2/25/2020

Contents

Chapter 1

DEATH BY BLACK HOLE

In January 2019, astronomers were watching distant galaxies with different kinds of telescopes. A network of telescopes on Earth looked for supernovas, or exploding stars. Out in space, an orbiting telescope looked for exoplanets, or planets outside our solar system. One of the telescopes on Earth saw a bright flash of light in a far-off galaxy, 375 million light-years from Earth. Was it a supernova?

This illustration shows a strange space object. What could it be?

A BLACK HOLE WILL SUCK UP THE GASES OF A NEARBY STAR IF THE STAR GETS TOO CLOSE.

▼

The astronomers running the telescopes took a closer look. The telescopes on Earth, part of the All-Sky Automated Survey for Supernovae (ASAS-SN), all focused on the flash in the sky. The space telescope, the Transiting Exoplanet Survey Satellite (TESS), took a closer look too. Soon the astronomers figured out what they were looking at. The flash was not coming from a supernova. It was from a star that had wandered too close to a black hole.

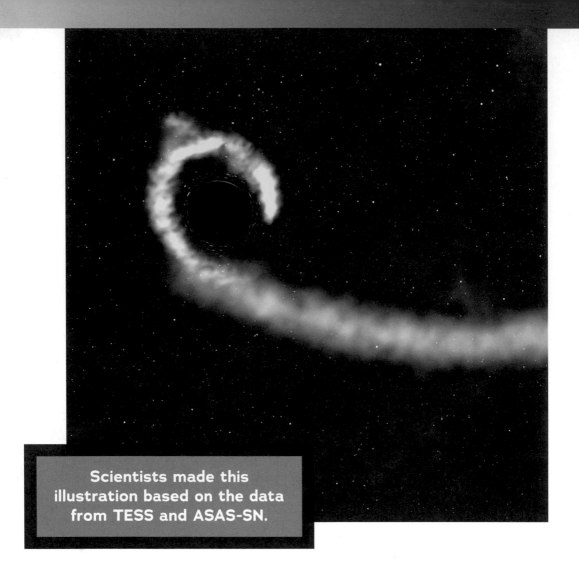

Scientists made this illustration based on the data from TESS and ASAS-SN.

The End Is Near

If a star gets too close to a black hole, it is doomed. The black hole's powerful gravity will rip the star to shreds. As the star comes apart, its gases swirl around the edges of the black hole like water running down a drain. Some of the gases disappear into the black hole. Other gases shoot off into space like fireworks.

That's what happened in January 2019. Astronomers had seen black holes eating stars before. But ASAS-SN and TESS gave them a closer and more detailed view of this event than ever before. Pictures from the telescopes showed the star's hot gases swirling around the black hole and shooting into space.

Telescopes and other high-tech equipment have helped astronomers learn a lot about black holes. But they have much more to learn.

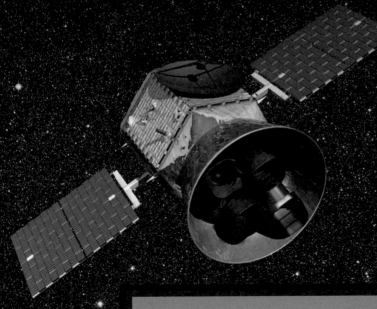

TESS was launched in 2018 with a two-year mission to help astronomers find planets outside of our own solar system.

Chapter 2

NO ESCAPE

Black holes are mysterious for many reasons. For one thing, we can't see them. A black hole is an area in space with so much gravity that nothing can escape its pull. Not even light can escape a black hole, and something that doesn't reflect or give off light is invisible.

A black hole might look like a dark circle, but scientists don't know for sure.

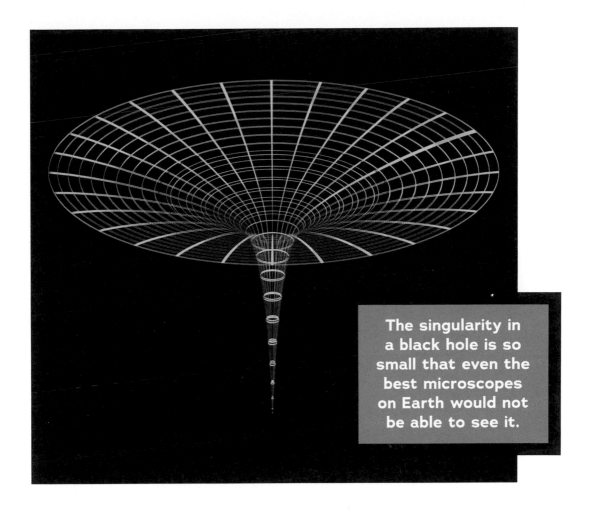

The singularity in a black hole is so small that even the best microscopes on Earth would not be able to see it.

What's inside a black hole? At its center is a point called the singularity. The point is smaller than an atom, but enormous amounts of matter are squeezed into it. Some singularities have more matter than a million suns. All that matter squeezed into such a tiny space creates extreme gravity. That's why nothing can escape a black hole.

A BLACK HOLE'S STRONG GRAVITY CAN BEND LIGHT.

▼

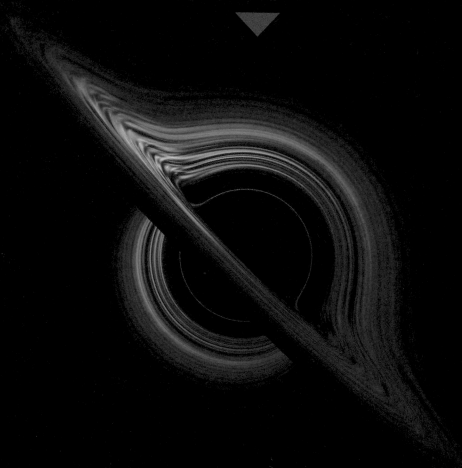

Point of No Return

The outer edge of a black hole is called the event horizon. The event horizon is like a boundary line for gravity. Inside the event horizon, a black hole's gravity is too strong for even light to escape.

When a star wanders close to a black hole, it speeds up. Scientists have found a star orbiting a black hole at a speed of 8 million miles (13 million km) per hour!

Lots of stars orbit black holes at a safe distance. But occasionally a star travels too close to a black hole and crosses the event horizon. Then there's no turning back. The black hole rips the star to pieces and devours most of its gases. Black holes also eat dust, planets, and any other objects that cross their event horizons.

Mystery Holes

Scientists think that everything that falls into a black hole becomes part of the singularity, adding to the black hole's powerful gravity. But scientists aren't really sure what happens inside a black hole. Many scientists think the rules of physics don't apply there. They think time might even slow down or stop inside a black hole.

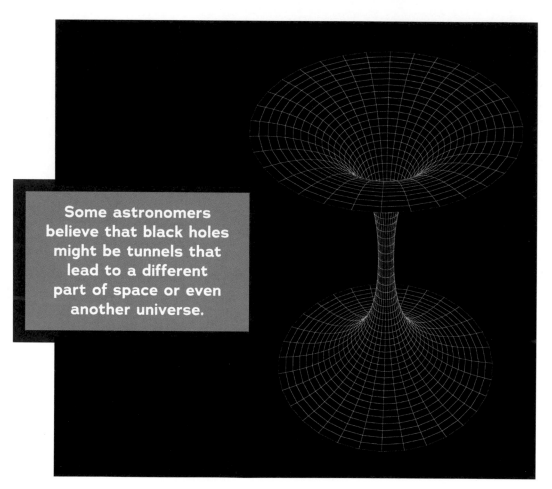

Some astronomers believe that black holes might be tunnels that lead to a different part of space or even another universe.

STEM Spotlight

In 1974, British physicist Stephen Hawking (*below*) proposed that black holes give off tiny particles that take away their energy. Physicists call this process Hawking radiation. If Hawking's theory is correct, then black holes will gradually lose mass and eventually disappear. But no one knows for sure whether Hawking radiation really exists. By studying black holes, physicists hope to find the facts.

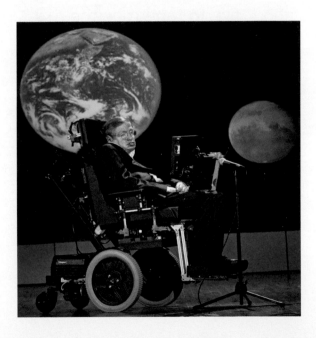

Chapter 3

SIZING UP BLACK HOLES

The universe has billions of black holes. The most common ones are called stellar black holes. *Stellar* means "star." Stellar black holes started out as stars. Then they exploded as supernovas and their centers collapsed, pulled inward by their own gravity. Most stellar black holes have about five to ten times the mass of our sun.

A stellar black hole forms at the center of the cloud of gas and dust left over from an exploding star.

Supermassive black holes are just that: supermassive. Their masses can be millions or even billions of times greater than the mass of our sun. Astronomers think that every galaxy has a supermassive black hole at its center. The supermassive black hole at the center of the Milky Way, our galaxy, is called Sagittarius A*.

SAGITTARIUS A* HAS ABOUT 4.5 MILLION TIMES MORE MASS THAN OUR SUN.

Astronomers aren't sure how supermassive black holes form. One theory is that stellar black holes grow larger and larger over billions of years. By swallowing stars and merging with other black holes, they eventually become supermassive. Another theory says that supermassive black holes were supermassive from the start. They took shape when giant clouds of gas and dust collapsed during the formation of the first galaxies.

When a black hole consumes material, it lets out powerful jets. Scientists want to find out what causes the jets.

Looking for More

Stellar and supermassive black holes aren't the only kinds of black holes. Intermediate-mass black holes are larger than stellar black holes and smaller than supermassive black holes. They probably form when stellar black holes collide and join together. But astronomers have found only a few intermediate-mass black holes, so we don't know much about them.

The purple dot near the bottom of this image of a galaxy shows where scientists think there might be an intermediate-mass black hole.

Chapter 4

SEEING THE INVISIBLE

Since black holes are invisible, astronomers cannot see them directly. But materials swirling around a black hole's event horizon give off light and energy.

All the black holes that we know about are much too far away to pull on our sun.

The swirling material around black holes orbits very quickly. The speed causes the material to heat up and give off light.

Astronomers can use telescopes to detect X-rays, radio waves, infrared waves, and other types of energy coming from materials swirling around black holes. When astronomers find these swirls of energy, they know they have discovered a black hole.

This illustration shows gravitational waves rippling across space as two black holes approach each other.

Prepare to Merge

What happens when two black holes crash into each other? They merge to create a bigger, more powerful black hole with more gravity and mass. Something else happens when black holes collide. They send gravitational waves rippling through space.

About 1.3 billion years ago, two stellar black holes collided and merged. Each one was about thirty times as massive as our sun. The collision created superstrong waves of gravity. They spread through space like ocean waves. By the time they reached Earth, the waves had lost most of their energy and were so tiny that people didn't feel them.

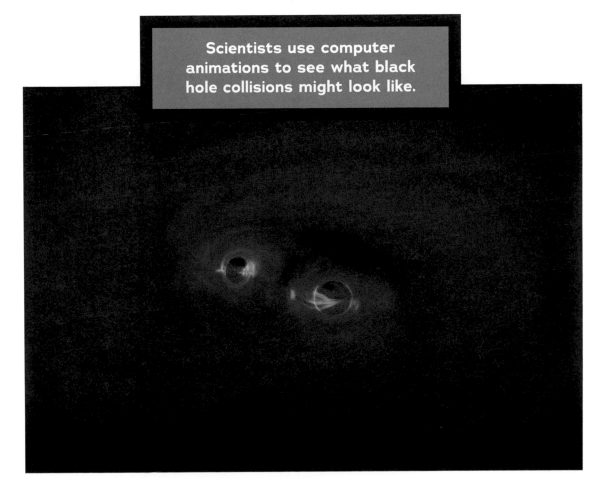

Scientists use computer animations to see what black hole collisions might look like.

The timing was perfect. The Laser Interferometer Gravitational-Wave Observatory (LIGO) had just opened in Louisiana and Washington. LIGO uses giant, supersensitive antennas to detect gravitational waves. Scientists at LIGO recorded, measured, and studied the waves coming from the black hole collision. Since then, LIGO has detected more gravitational waves. LIGO will help astronomers learn more about supermassive black holes.

The LIGO antennas use supersensitive lasers buried underground to detect gravitational waves.

The charts on the computer screens in this picture show data from the two LIGO detectors. Both detectors sensed the same gravitational wave.

The Big Picture

In April 2019, a team of astronomers made an exciting announcement. As part of a project called the Event Horizon Telescope, they had taken a picture of a black hole's event horizon. They were ready to show it to the world.

The Event Horizon Telescope is actually made up of many telescopes from around the world. One of those telescopes is the Atacama Large Millimeter/submillimeter Array (ALMA) in Chile.

You can't take a picture of a black hole with an ordinary camera because black holes are invisible. But the astronomers didn't use an ordinary camera. Instead, they used radio telescopes located in different places on Earth. The telescopes had all collected radio waves coming from gases and stars swirling around a supermassive black hole at the center of a galaxy called Messier 87.

STEM Spotlight

One billion light-years from Earth, three supermassive black holes (*shown in the box below*) are on track to collide. When the black holes crash in about a billion years, the energy from the collision will send some stars flying out of their galaxies. Other stars will be swallowed by the supermassive black holes. The three galaxies that surround the supermassive black holes will combine—with an even more massive black hole at the center.

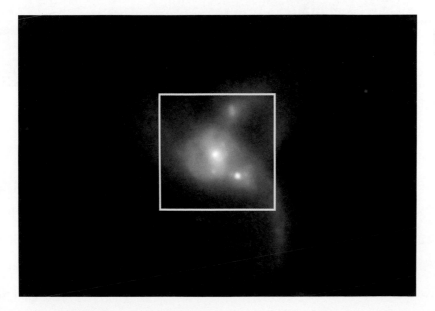

The photo taken by the Event Horizon Telescope shows the event horizon glowing around the black hole's shadow.

Scientists combined the signals gathered by the ten radio telescopes and converted them into an image. It shows a glowing orange doughnut shape with a black spot at its center. The center is the black hole. The doughnut shape is the hot, glowing material spinning around the black hole's event horizon. The astronomers had taken the first-ever photograph of a black hole's event horizon. Astronomers want to make pictures of more black holes. These pictures will help us solve more mysteries about black holes.

3D Printer Activity

TESS captured images of a black hole eating a star in 2019. To download instructions for making a 3D-printed model of the telescope, visit the below link.

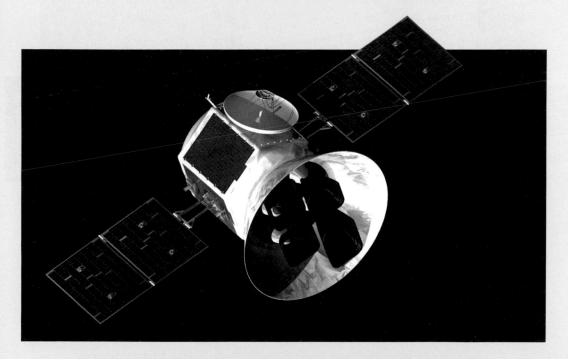

PAGE PLUS+

https://qrs.lernerbooks.com/TESS

Glossary

astronomer: a scientist who studies objects and matter in space

event horizon: the border beyond which light cannot escape a black hole's gravity

galaxy: a vast system of stars, planets, dust, gases, and other matter in space, all held together by gravity

gravitational wave: a type of energy created by violent events, such as the collision of two black holes. The waves ripple through space at the speed of light.

gravity: an invisible force that attracts stars, planets, and other objects to one another. The more massive an object is, the stronger its gravity is.

light-year: the distance that light travels in one year. One light-year equals about 5.88 trillion miles (9.46 trillion km).

mass: the amount of matter in an object

matter: the material an object is made of

merge: to join together as one

orbit: to travel around something in circles

physics: the science that deals with matter, energy, and how they behave and interact

singularity: the tiny point at the very center of a black hole

Learn More about Black Holes

Books

Doeden, Matt. *Albert Einstein: Relativity Rock Star*. Minneapolis: Lerner
    Publications, 2020.
    Physicist Albert Einstein developed theories about space, time,
    energy, gravity, and matter. He set the stage for the study of black
    holes and other objects.

Galat, Joan Marie. *Space*. Washington, DC: National Geographic Kids, 2020.
    This book explores the far reaches of space to teach you about
    supernovas, black holes, and more.

Kurtz, Kevin. *Cutting-Edge Black Holes Research*. Minneapolis: Lerner
    Publications, 2020.
    Learn about black holes and how scientists study these massive,
    invisible space objects.

Websites

Black Holes
    https://www.esa.int/kids/en/learn/Our_Universe/Story_of_the_Universe
    /Black_Holes
    This website from the European Space Agency explains black holes
    and gives links to other space topics.

Milky Way Galaxy
    https://kids.nationalgeographic.com/explore/space/milky-way/
    Our galaxy is a vast collection of stars and other objects with
    a supermassive black hole at the center. Learn about the Milky
    Way here.

What Is a Gravitational Wave?
    https://spaceplace.nasa.gov/gravitational-waves/en/
    This website explains what a gravitational wave is and how LIGO
    detected them.

Index

Photo Acknowledgments

Image credits: NASA/JPL-Caltech, p. 4; NASA/CXC/M.Weiss, p. 5; NASA/Goddard Space Flight Center, pp. 6, 16, 23; NASA/ESA/Digitized Sky Survey 2, Acknowledgment ESA/Hubble (Davide De Martin), p. 7; brightstars/iStock/Getty Images, p. 8; local_doctor/Shutterstock.com, p. 9; NASA/Goddard Space Flight Center/Jeremy Schnittman, p. 10; ESA/Hubble, M. Kornmesser (CC BY 4.0), p. 11; YuLi4ka/iStock/Getty Images, p. 12; NASA/Paul E. Alers, p. 13; Chandra X-ray Observatory, pp. 14, 15; X-ray: NASA/CXC/UNH/D. Lin et al.; Optical: NASA/ESA/STScI, p. 17; ESO/L. Cal (CC BY 4.0), p. 18; ESO/M. Kornmesser (CC BY 4.0), p. 19; X-ray: NASA/CXC/INAF/A. Wolter et al. Optical: NASA/STScI, p. 20; NASA, ESA, Martin Kornmesser (ESA/Hubble), p. 21; NASA/C. Henze, p. 22; Caltech/MIT/LIGO Lab, p. 24; PhilipNeustrom/Wikimedia Commons (public domain), p. 25; ESO/C. Malin (CC BY 4.0), p. 26; X-ray: NASA/CXC/George Mason University/R. Pfeifle et al.; Optical: SDSS & NASA/STScI, p. 27; Event Horizon Telescope Collaboration, p. 28; alejomiranda/iStock/Getty Images, p. 29.

Cover: ESO/M. Kornmesser (CC BY 4.0).